Iain Si[n]...
thirty y[ears]...
second-hand book-dealer, a ...
documentary film maker. His most recent book, *Rodinsky's Room*, written with Rachel Lichtenstein, was published to great acclaim. As well as *Sorry Meniscus* – his diatribe on the Millennium Dome – Sinclair's other books on London include *Liquid City* and *Lights Out for the Territory*. His novels include *Downriver*, which won the Encore Award and the James Tait Black Memorial Prize, *Lud Heat* and *Radon Daughters*. He writes regularly for the *London Review of Books* and has presented films and documentary features for both TV and radio.

Sorry Meniscus

Excursions to the Millennium Dome

IAIN SINCLAIR

P

PROFILE BOOKS

in association with

LONDON REVIEW OF BOOKS

First published
in book form in Great Britain in 1999 by
PROFILE BOOKS LTD
58a Hatton Garden, London EC1N 8LX
www.profilebooks.co.uk

Previously published in part in 1999 by
LONDON REVIEW OF BOOKS
28 Little Russell Street, London WC1A 2HN
www.lrb.co.uk

Typeset in Quadraat
Designed by Peter Campbell
Printed and bound in Great Britain by
St Edmundsbury Press, Bury St Edmunds

A CIP catalogue record for this book is available
from the British Library.
ISBN 1 86197 179 6

Crunching over the shingle, beneath Folly Wall on the eastern shore of the Isle of Dogs, at first light on an early summer morning, the Dome shines across the leaden water like a brilliant shell. This is a setting that deserves to be recognised as one of J.G. Ballard's terminal beaches: the last council-operated high-rise block behind me and an unscripted future ahead, the yellow-spiked Teflon tent like a genetically modified mollusc. It's a fossil from some provisional era that will never have to be lived through in anything beyond virtual reality. I've lost all sense of scale, time itself is on the drift. In my rucksack is the most convincing evidence that this dome is something other than a low octane hallucination: a photographic memento from the early days of the project, from 22nd June 1997. London as a millennial landscape, scoured, bone dry, without dust or dirt or atmosphere. The East Greenwich Peninsula as Cape Canaveral; a launch pad for a range of super-celestial blues. Toxic marshlands, the residue of defunct gas works, transformed by the swipe of a mouse to Florida. I hold up the promotional photograph against its pale twin. And realise that this is how the whole millennium scam should have been worked. The 'computer-generated realisation', produced by Hayes Davidson for the New Millennium Experience Company, is better, grander, more visionary than anything New Labour will achieve by dumping something close to a billion pounds into the deadlands.

What a fabulous album this is. Put these images on a screen and they could evolve, shift, *breathe*, like M.R. James's mezzotint. I mean that staring at this unpeopled, radiant city would be to imagine movement, pick up on spectral traces; to treat this flat rectangle of card like a scrying glass or crystal ball. The curved sky hymns perpetual morning. White tails of steepling wash from riverboats emphasise the sweep of Limehouse Reach. This is London as seen from a returning space shuttle; a vision of privilege, limitless budgets, a cure for cancer. The hubris of the Canary

Wharf tower is modified by casting the building in shadow, allowing bands of morning light to pick out patches of lush greenery, the depths and currents of a tropical Thames. Delirious fictions. How much more feasible this whole millennial extravaganza would be as a laptop fantasy. The Dome as Hayes Davidson have presented it makes all that tedious construction work, all the blocked roads and discontinued river paths, all the site traffic, the rows and resignations, unnecessary. Redundant. In these advance Polaroids of something that will never happen, the steel needles from which the tent will be slung are black or white (not the final yellow), and the Dome is blocked in by paddocks of neatly parked cars (a notion that was soon to be rejected). It's quite obvious, or so it seemed to me, that the answer to all this fuss is to erect marquees on village greens and in municipal parks, hand out free virtual reality headsets. Let us all enjoy the Dome trip, its splendours and excesses, without having to organise an expedition to the Peninsula. Scrub the building work, the frantic teams of conceptualisers and persuaders. Get it all over with in a weekend.

The primary symbol, this low mound or sugary dune, was half-right. What was horribly wrong was the making manifest of an emblem that should have been left as a metaphor, a signature for the designers. The quarrels between Stephen Bayley as image broker and Peter Mandelson as Dome Czar ('single shareholder') were an inevitable consequence of parallel but irreconcilable versions of the world. Bayley gave the impression that he would have been happier if the whole 'experience' could have been shifted to the Design Museum that he had launched with Sir Terence Conran, a few miles upstream near Tower Bridge. Mandelson, on the other hand, the master of consensus politics, required the Dome to shapeshift, become all things to all men. It didn't exist as a fixed point on the geography of London. It was theoretical. He had commissioned these advance portraits and he damned reality to contradict him.

So there it was, meaningless and magnificent, a pale intruder on the downriver mud. Alien plunder washed ashore on a rogue tide. Blocking out the memory of discontinued industry, the Dome is a blob of congealed correction fluid, a flick of Tipp-Ex to revise the mistakes of 19th-century industrialists. What could not be revised, and what drifted across the water on a light breeze, were the ancient stinks, the 'corrosive vapours' that made East Greenwich infamous: molasses, guano, bad sugar. Borges' famous description of the Falklands War had been turned inside out: here was the bald head that the two men had been fighting over, tines of a steel comb buried in a silvery scalp. But that didn't invalidate the symbol, the cosmic ring. The problem was that the circuit of the Dome covered nothing and meant whatever its sponsors said that it meant. It abducted poetry and pressed it into service for a form of debased copywriting. The chemically enhanced skin of the Dome was as tight as a repeat-order facelift. Trump's bump.

As I left oozing footprints in the mud at the water's edge, brooding on the greed, the millennial madness that this date change had engendered, I wondered if the curry house behind me, with its view across the river, was already booked solid for the big night. Every pub and rat hole between Dartford and Rotherhithe seemed to be getting in on the act. Prices had trebled. Bar staff, quite reasonably, were demanding quadruple overtime. For what? A few fireworks and a posse of freeloaders having a good time in a tent. The PR campaign had already begun to pay off, with hireling journos and rent-a-gob hacks falling into line. Born-again Dome Moonies were everywhere. 'I'm backing the Bump' was about to become the hip metropolitan attitude; a last days of the Roman Empire stunt. Compulsively rehydrating on middle-range plonk in an exotic location where they had never previously bothered to get out of the car, mew-mewing the same faces they see every night on the circuit, the whole deal seemed to make sense. Just another launch with a proper budget. Simon Jenkins, 'millennial commissar', and 'two-hundred odd heavy friends' (as one of them, John Walsh, put it in the *Independent*) laying on a great party for the movers and shakers. 'The Dome is brilliant,' Walsh duly delivered. 'It's very white … We had more chardonnay … Here was £700m-worth spent on a celebration of present, past and future … And here was the cream of London society, struggling to take it seriously.'

I couldn't go that far, but I had to admit that this shape, the Dome, had its resonance. What if a dome could be stretched over the area circumscribed by the M25? A caul of translucent skin. A Blakean conceit, fierce, true, but held only in the mind. Demanding no dole, no lottery tax, no road closures, no design consultants, no sweetheart deals, no drudging out to a stub of poisoned land. Coleridge's opium dream invoked 'the shadow of the dome of pleasure' that 'floated midway on the waves'. The Dome as a conceit, an emblem lifted into the consciousness of all those who lived inside its limits. An instant of good will, a breath, a caesura between centuries. That's my modest proposal. Stick with the visions of the computer-enhanced riverscapes, the celestial cities with their parks and forests and fountains. Imagine the Dome as it ought to be, rather than as it is: a poached egg designed by a committee of vegans.

The transformation had been so swift. Early in the year, I set out from the Dome, with photographer Marc Atkins and author (ex-KLF) Bill Drummond, to walk, as nearly as we could, up the line of zero longitude. I'd been invited by the *London Review of Books*, back in 1997, to report on a site visit, a tour of inspection, paddling across the turned-over topsoil that would soon be covered by Teflon-coated canvas. Drummond has the reputation (not something he takes any trouble to cultivate) of being a very serious prankster. He's the man who, with Jimmy Cauty, awarded the anti-Turner prize (worth more than the official version) to Rachel Whiteread. He's the one who burnt a million quid and then, a mistake in my opinion, allowed a home-video of the event to run around the fringes as a well-attended perfor-mance piece. Drummond and the putative Dome belonged together. The man, it's obvious, is a kind of displaced Non-Conformist missionary, determined to exorcise (by repetition if neces-sary) the karma of his Scottish inheritance, all those bible-in-the-fist colonists. He's good com-pany as a walker, up to speed on flora and fauna – magpies, herons, all species of crow, the twist in chestnut trees as they respond to the passage of sunlight. Drummond is carrying, and quoting from, a copy of The Unabomber Manifesto. He's so stone-cold sane (with a laugh that strips bark from the willows), so intense in his pursuit of tactics that might make the world bearable, that I begin to believe he'd be crazy enough to hire a chopper and napalm this preposterous tent. He's already admitted that he'd like to command a fleet of earth-movers that would turn over all the standing stones on Salisbury Plain. The Dome, as he glowers at it, stepping from his minicab on Dreadnought Street, trembles. The steel supports are an Anthony Caro reprise of Stonehenge. A place of power that has to be disguised like one of those permanently shrinkwrapped City developments, hidden beneath shivering polythene bandages. Back in Spitalfields, grave robbery can be kept from prying eyes. There's a neat canvas igloo to protect the excavation of a Roman coffin from a building site where office development will soon dominate the old fruit and vegetable market, and overshadow the famous view, looking east, from Bishopsgate towards Nicholas Hawksmoor's Christ Church.

Tents in the mud. Tents surrounded by yellow and blue tape. Men in hardhats, gumboots. Men with clipboards. Young women hefting video cameras. Uniformed personnel with digital recorders and spiral-bound notebooks. Perimeter fences and high density surveillance coverage. Pictures of guard dogs to warn off the illiterate. We expect them to be unearthing an atrocity. We have been well-schooled by television. We know more about pathology, rectal thermometers, wound profiles, the pigmentation of bruises, the speed at which maggots multiply in human meat, than is good for us. Rain is compulsory. Tents protect our sensibilities. In more fastidious times, only card-carrying initiates were granted access. Professionals. But now that veil has been torn aside. We've seen it all and learnt to distrust the carefully rehearsed banalities of the press conference, the ranking copper with his over-considered hair and his too bright suit.

Tents are for holes in the ground. Corrective surgery on the mantle of the city. Conan Doyle's Professor Challenger burrowing down to the centre of the earth. Tents provide cover for unexploded bombs left over from the Blitz. For leaking gas pipes. The hideous domestic butcheries of serial killers. Potential museum-quality sarcophagi or Elizabethan timbers disclosed during the clearance of another chunk of troublesome river frontage. The tent on the East Greenwich Peninsula had to be hiding something. Distracting the punters with a shining white handkerchief that will, at the optimum moment, be whipped away to reveal... They didn't know what. But they did know when. That was the bind. At the death, of course, they'd fall back, as ever, on William Blake. Blake is very useful – as a supplier of alternate national anthems, obscure pronouncements that can be spun any way the conceptualisers want them to go. A tacky circus with moth-eaten aerialists can present itself as a cosmic ballet in the high forest of night, 'bright angelic wings bespangling every bough like stars'. When the New Millennium Experience pulled Blake from under the hat, that was when I knew the game was up.

First Visit to the Millennium Experience Site:
September 1, 1997

Now we know, but back in September 1997, when the LRB offered me the chance of a sneak preview, I had no idea how the millennium project would develop. I had nothing to carry with me to the fenced-off site but my prejudices and a justified paranoia, polished by years of drifting about underimagined zones that were not-quite-London. Like everybody else I'd been subjected to a steady drip of news management and misinformation. The Dome was a classic Tory scam, a pointless but vaguely patriotic symbol sprayed over with cheerleader slogans. 'Rejoice.' Another replay of the old gravedigger's hymn. Happy-clappy imperialism. Cynics and the moderately under-enthused were denounced as party poopers and whingeing lefties. Rejoice. But what was left to celebrate in Mogadon Britain, with its beggars (native and imported), its hospitals converted into Wendy House estates, its care-in-the-community psychotics forced to discover that 'community' had evaporated somewhere around 1953, its failing inner city schools, its buggered-up legal system (enjoying more miscarriages than the most inbred royal broodmare), its Virgin ghost trains stalled somewhere outside Milton Keynes, its public clowns, unholy fools, craven press, zombie culture, and state-sponsored know-nothings? Who cares? Rejoice anyway. New Labour, after a few misgivings, was ready to pick up the tab. Opinion formers and massagers of statistics went into action. It was suggested that TV soap operas should slip in positive references to the Millennium Experience and arrange, budget permitting, day trips to East Greenwich. The credits for *EastEnders* might be revised, so that the location of the Dome would be imprinted on the minds of submissive viewers.

I understood all that, but it still gets me every time. That hallucinatory instant. Da da da da da, da da. The Pearly Queen drill of the *EastEnders* signature tune, as the river map spins and the world is stood on its head; what you thought was the stump of the Isle of Dogs is revealed as the East Greenwich Peninsula. That same desperate readjustment of consciousness is what you face when you emerge, high on diesel fumes and road rage, from the tiled bore of the Blackwall Tunnel. There's no other way, with an appointment to keep at Gate 10 of the heavily protected Millennium Experience site, to get across the river from the north shore. What we could all use is another bridge, another tunnel, but that's not on the New Labour agenda. Too expensive, too much hassle. Too heavy, too Soviet. Too… pedestrian. There isn't the time, before the Big Day, to commission statistics, collate opinions, take soundings. Far better to stick with the blank canvas, a curved white screen on which anything can be projected. That's what the Dome is, a potential drive-past cinema (twinned with similar venues on the Southend Road, chunks of *faux*-Americana in Dagenham). Stunning images, product placement, faces of the plastic gods, will be cast onto the taught skin of the Dome. They'll be silent. They won't have anything to say. The message is no message. Look and wonder.

Blinking from the half-light of the Blackwall Tunnel, it's evident that nobody crosses water without paying a price. There is ample evidence of the alien otherness that north-bankers fear when forced to make this short transit, dim marshlands giving way to the skeletal remains of the South Metropolitan Gas Works. The writer and musician Jah Wobble remembers his days driving minicabs, ferrying razor-striped Whitechapel faces south of the river for regular bits of business, cash drops. These awesomely fragrant knuckle-breakers would sit, sweating into their savage suits, molesting the scarlet leather, until they made it safely back through the tunnel. They would pile into the nearest boozer and throw back doubles until they could lift a shot glass without spilling half its contents.

The ride to the tunnel haunts Kray foot-soldier Tony Lambrianou. He replays it like a psychogeographical nightmare: Evering Road, Lower Clapton Road, Narrow Way, Mare Street, Cambridge Heath Road, Commercial Road, East India Dock Road. The site on the Greenwich Peninsula nominated for national celebration, after outflanking a rival proposal from Birmingham, was once the resting place of the mummified-in-an-Axminster cadaver of Jack 'The Hat' McVitie (the famous for being dead villain). This sinister wasteland, first left out of the tunnel, just past the gas holder, demarcated the limits of Lambrianou's imagination. It was as far from Hackney as he ever wanted to travel.

But all those dubious urban myths have been forgotten and forgiven. This is now, the dawn of a new millennium. The carcinogenic venom of the Greenwich marshes has been painlessly neutralised. They have received the blessing of Tony Blair. This shabby field of dreams is where Britain will show the world how to have a good time by erecting the most expensive tent in the universe. As the Minister Without Portfolio, Peter Mandelson, asserts in a document issued from the Cabinet Office: 'millenniums only come once in a thousand years'. Or at approximately the same interval as Labour governments with a mandate to do whatever they want, with absolutely no comeback, in the wake of the Tory meltdown and the merciful extinction of the sorriest rump of chancers, carpetbaggers, and self-serving pondlife ever inflicted on a masochistic democracy.

The relish with which I looked forward to my site visit was seasoned with a pinch of guilt. Everything I knew and everything I had found out about the New Millennium Experience confirmed it as the sort of mistake which would haunt a government for generations. The very name had the authentic whiff of disaster – like the South Sea Bubble, the Stavisky Affair, the Profumo Scandal. But on a much grander scale, gonzo hubris. They'd dragged time itself into the equation. The short-termism, the lack of vision, was so obvious. This fenced-off paddock was a triumph of doublespeak, boasting of ecological benefits while ordering an indestructible PVC dome (later downgraded to Teflon); banging on about the river, while ensuring that Thames walkers have to make a massive detour that carries them far inland; banning cars for trippers while clogging the Blackwall Tunnel with lorryloads of glow-in-the-dark topsoil. How could you acclaim a people's park that was guarded like a penal colony? Could anywhere that had been so universally and repeatedly ridiculed by the media be all bad? (How long would it be before editors were brought into line?) Was there some creepier anti-Mandelson (anti-Semitic) conspiracy abroad? Anyone in these pre-millennial days who wasn't a fully paid-up conspiracy freak wasn't trying.

To fix the details of my site visit, I'd had to work my way from the 'media desk' at the Cabinet Office to English Partnerships' own answering service. It was hard to find a good day to talk. But that's the culture now, being held in a queue while you wait for some disembodied voice to guide you through the latest crash on your word processor. Hours drift, your head filling up with water-torture muzak. Unfortunate glitches in the smooth progress of news management were getting in the way of my appointment. First there was the eco lobby who had alerted the press to the fact that the skin of the Dome would, like Cat Woman's suit, be made from PVC; German PVC. 'Softeners', which might also be 'hormone disrupters', were mentioned, as well as stabilisers of cadmium or lead. A trip to the Big Top might be altogether too millennial, gifting you with a pharmacopoeia of tissue-devouring mutations. A consensus was arrived at: PVC with its lethal dioxins would be replaced by Teflon, the house-wife's friend. A seven or eight million quid sweet-ner would buy off the Germans. Mandelson, the Kubla Khan of New Labour, who had been elo-quent in defence of the original material of choice, was now equally enthused by its under-study. Once that diversion was out of the way the Dome think-tank could get back to deciding what the Big Idea was going to be, the secret of the tent within a tent, a 'Drum' that would hold 10,000 spectators. Perhaps they should consider a giant grey homburg, commissioned from Claes Olden-burg, in memory of Jack McVitie?

Mr Terence Gibbons, the media facilitator de-puted to show off the absence of sights, was affa-ble, and he was on time. He'd warned me about the tight security cordon. (There's no better way of making a hole in the ground important than by giving it the full Rushdie.) Simply having 'your name on the gate' was no guarantee of access. During earlier expeditions I'd been turned away by a one-eyed gateman who had strayed from an underfunded production of *Macbeth*. (Most of the Greenwich theatres, civic and pub backroom, were closing for lack of grant aid.) Today a cheery West African contented himself with sending me back to find a car. Ownership of a vehicle was the best proof of serious intent. There was no question of walking in off the road. Pedestrians were potential terrorists.

Lifting the barrier at Gate 10, the security man instructed me to drive straight ahead without deviation, keeping my eyes on the road. I'd find Mr Gibbons waiting at Gate 3A. And, sure enough, in leather jacket, dark glasses, with mobile at the ready, there he was.

Kitted out in baby-blue hard hats, Tweetie Pie waistcoats, we were travestied for a photo opportunity that would never arrive. As we picked our way over the impacted dust, the hot conglomerate, I wondered if I'd been a bit hasty in turning down the rubber boots. Too late. The problem was that if you weren't here for a publicity snapshot, there was nowhere to go. Civilians visited East Greenwich to be seen rather than to see. It was a location backdrop announcing: Enterprise, Investment, Action. The hardhat matched with

pinstripe suit (or white boilersuit and Chieftain tank) were key icons of the Thatcher era. Getaway limos, engines purring, kept just out of frame. The brownfield photo shoot was another Tory idea that New Labour had decided to recycle. *Millennium (The Newsletter of the Millennium Experience)*, an ersatz theatre programme, featured Sir Cameron Mackintosh on one cover and the posing reservoir dogs of the Labour front bench on the other. Uniform dark grey suits (no retrospective pinstripes), blue helmets, trout stream wellies and – apart from John Prescott – full zip millennial grins. The long-focus lens tactfully blurs the backdrop of industrial dereliction. Britain is working. Hands-on management. Optimism. Good humour. (Flashbacks to Neil Kinnock's famous tumble in the shallows on Brighton beach are strictly verboten.)

Here's how Mr Gibbons pitches it. Employment. Dole bandits rounded up in a depressed area. The Jubilee Line extension. Life returning to a dead river. The defiant and cavalier spirit of free enterprise. They said the Great Exhibition was a waste of money. They said the Festival of Britain wouldn't pull the punters. This is a signal to the world: we can transform vision into reality in the shortest possible space of time. Give us the bread and we'll give you the circuses. In twenty-eight months from depressed marshland to a Barnum and Bailey showground. 'And the vision is?' I asked. 'Er, time,' Mr Gibbons replied. 'Time,' he repeated, after a significant pause, remembering to capitalise the abstraction. I understood: millennium, zero longitude, Greenwich. Prospects for future sport-fests. Berlin in the Thirties, without Leni Reifenstahl. Two hundred million pounds of lottery tax is small change when set against the conceptual brilliance, the dynamism of this proposal.

You can almost believe it. The site is buzzing. The great yellow struts on which the Dome will be erected are lying on their sides like decommissioned ordnance. Piles are being driven deep into the clay. There are more caravans than on Canvey Island. The inconvenience of the white funnel that disperses the exhaust fumes from the Blackwall Tunnel will soon be hidden away. Mischievous journalists have suggested that the Dome will envelop this funnel, turning the tent into a killing zone, a voluntary euthanasia facility. That would be in the true spirit of the millennium: suicide cults, comet-watchers, surfers of the Book of Revelations. Alas, it's not so. The fat white lips will poke clear of the Teflon. You won't even see them in the official portraits, the pristine virtual reality handouts.

But you'll smell the fumes. An unmannerly belch of black smoke. A brewery pall that hits you as soon as you emerge from the Blackwall Tunnel: oasty, hot in the throat, disquieting. Griddled bird shit. The world through a sepia filter. Dust-storms of gravy browning. Iron filings in a furious wind scrape the cornea. Noise you can taste. The thump of generators and jack-hammers refusing to synchronise with your heart-beat. Headache preambles. The torrid promise of 'Peter's Savoury Products.' Yards decorated with Hazchem drums in the same virulently on-message blue as the millennial hardhats. Greenwich Peninsula is the home of Amylum UK (Glucose, Starches, Proteins); of the Byphosphated Guano Company, manufacturers of 'artificial manure';

of the Molassine Works, makers of animal foods ('Vims – all dogs love it'); of Harrison Barber's knackers' yard. (Those lovely old dobbins you noticed out on the marshes are waiting their turn for the stungun.)

Sheltering in Dreadnought Street, bent against back-draughts from tailgating traffic, you can admire a startling dystopian panorama of auto-fetishism, chemical alps, flame-holders burning off waste products, and an ever-changing hoarding that dwarfs Dorrington's, a joke-Tudor barn of a pub. The hoarding announces a new film release: *Conspiracy Theory*. The pub forecourt, inches from the tunnel access road, is ankle-deep in broken bottles – Liebfraumilch Pflaz, Olde English, the Original Strong Cyder, Beck's Beer, Omega Extra Strong White Cider, Dragon Stout. Nights here are given over to 'playing Garage, Speed Garage, Deep America House'. The landscape fizzes, spits, coughs. It's cooking itself in a thermal casserole. Even the graffiti on the concrete walkway seems to have been provided by a sympathetic set-dresser: 'Disorientate Yourself. Reappropriate Your Surroundings.'

This is a place of miraculous transformations, metempsychosis. We don't need the tent, we're already inhabiting an invisible dome, an inverted bowl of protein soup (courtesy of Hays Chemicals) in which new life forms are breeding and taking shape.

I got along pretty well with Mr Gibbons, as you do with people paid to show you a good time. The backslapping fellowship stemmed from the fact that we would, in all probability, never have to set eyes on each other again. He guided me to an elevated viewing platform, one of those temporary structures that look as if they've been thrown up as somewhere to take the salute for a passing out parade. I gave him my card. It says: 'Used Books'. And is handy for claiming discounts in second-hand bookshops. A few days later, Terence was on the phone. His bosses were searching for a copy of Bevis Hiller's *A Tonic for the Nation*. A little creative plagiarism was in order. They wanted to check out the Festival of Britain copywriters. And, standing on this platform, you could appreciate the fact that the Millennium Experience needed all the help it could get. The Peninsula site was under pressure, pressure of time; and the clock ('Mean Time by Accurist') moving remorselessly towards countdown, zero hour at zero longitude. And so, in the way that confidences pass between two strangers leaning on the parapet of a bridge, staring down into the maelstrom, Mr Gibbons let slip what his version of the Big Idea might be. A piss-up. A cusp of the millennium concert party. The Spice Girls. Oasis. A forklift of tenors. Sir Cliff Richard (there'd be no way of keeping him out of it). Negotiations were already underway. Who could turn down a prestigious gig at the end of the century with a budget that could blow away Las Vegas? (Gibbons hadn't considered the skull-splitting anthem recently performed by Bill Drummond and Jimmy Cauty, and their massed proletarian choruses, at the Barbican. I offered to show him the T-shirt. 'Fuck the Millennium.')

Dizzy on fumes from the tunnel, I began to see what he meant. It was the vision in the brochures that counted, virtual reality. The world as it should be, if only we could believe; demonstrate our faith in the sainted Blair. The blue river. The orchards. The gardens. If only we were capable of crawling under Jonathan Aitken's trusty shield of traditional British fair play, clearing this wilderness with his sword of truth. We'd much prefer to put our faith in the brochures and not the evidence of our eyes. Peter Mandelson assured us in the first line of his Cabinet Office pronouncement that 'the Prime Minister went to Greenwich, personally'. Instead of taking the easier option and making the trip in the Tardis? Too many visits had been written up, too many speeches reported, before they had taken place. Doubters began to wonder if Mandelson was a replicant. They froze their video tapes, trying to decide if all the muscles in his face were working as he spoke out of the side of his mouth, issued the latest denial. Modestly, Mandelson's title stressed the negative: Minister Without Portfolio. The man was a positive discrimination amputee. But the media jackals suggested that it wasn't the portfolio that had been carelessly lopped off but the prefix. 'Prime.' It was Mandelson who was running this show, ironing the stretchmarks from the Blair grin, convening sub-committees to rethink the

Chairman's haircut. The paranoia which seemed to underwrite Mandelson's self-confidence, his instant, spray-on charm, was the fear that this inherited Dome brief would find him out, carrying, as it did, the karma that shafted that other nearly-man, Michael Heseltine.

New Labour had so much riding on the tent show that an operator as shrewd as Mandelson, a man tuned to every shift in public opinion, was already beginning to see parallels with the hollow triumphalism of the Sheffield rally that did for Neil Kinnock. The decision once taken, to ride with the decelerating Tory pitch, there was no way out. You could, if you were cynical enough, see the Dome fiasco as a nicely laid snare, a long-term strategy to destroy the incoming government. The Conservatives knew they were washed up. They'd been staggering about for years in an entropy tango. What could be more effective than to boobytrap the rotting hulk that New Labour would inherit? Leaving them, up to the ankles, in a noxious swamp; a theme park extravaganza that would provide directorships for some of the faithful and investment prospects for all their patrons. This folly would soak up funds that would otherwise be wasted on keeping electoral promises, restoring schools and hospitals. The East Greenwich Peninsula celebration was the death rattle of Thatcherism. This was the idea that was no idea. The Zen art of packaging soap-bubbles, making macrame shapes out of fantasy budgets. This was classic Archer-speak: brusque denials press-released before any accusation has been made. The New Millennium Experience was a blank cheque framed in barbed wire. Welcome aboard to the roll call of soft allegiance operators: McAlpine, Laing, Nuttall, Saatchi. Welcome, Mark McCormack (of IMG Associates), the per-centaged fund raiser who will oversee lesser beauticians of cash, make-over quangos. Wel-come, nouveaux aristos: Lord Rogers, Sir Cameron Mackintosh. Welcome, masters of spectacle: the peevish designer Stephen Bayley and Ken Robinson (who Bayley glosses as 'in charge of lavatories, parking, visitor flow'). There are jobs here for all those who missed out on Channel 4, warm seats for Arts Council panjan-drums and reality benders. A place on the board for Bob Ayling, Chief Executive of British Airways. For Ian Ash, British Telcom's Director of Corporate Relations. For David Quarmby, Chairman of the British Tourist Authority and the English Tourist Board. The concept is to be bigger than big, a blockbuster musical set on a desert island (Andrew Lloyd-Webber's *Tempest* pastiche). The Dome thesis is something so new and adventurous that the language to describe it has not yet been invented. But what has slipped the corporate consciousness, in the rapture of contemplating this provisional future, is that there is already a major bug in the system. On the big day, at the precise instant when all the clocks on Greenwich Hill, all the millennial calendars, click up the first nanosecond of the new thousand-year highway, it's all going to go horribly wrong. Because, as an old computer programmer, now an osteopath, pointed out as he worked some damage limitation into my wonky knee, that's when the system will go ape. 'Don't fly,' he said. 'And don't, for pity's sake, submit to surgery.' Wages, pensions, direct debits, quadruple bypasses, flight control, tax systems: chaos. When the dials go back to zero, they won't know how to behave. Memory banks will be wiped. Colour will drain from all the computer-enhanced visions. Crocodiles will emerge from primal sludge. Wolf-men with laser beam eyes will crawl out of the ventilation shafts of the Blackwall Tunnel. Space-time will warp and bend.

This will be the moment to readdress Norman Cohn's Sixties bed-sitter classic, *The Pursuit of the Millennium*. We'll understand that crossing the border between thousand-year cycles requires a proper dose of awe and terror. The end of a millennium is not to be carelessly celebrated by a Disneyland trade fair, nor exploited as well-disguised land speculation that will tart up dead ground for a future sell-off when property values in the neighbourhood have been boosted into the stratosphere. This should be a respite, a time of quiet contemplation. A time for the re-invention of history. Cohn speaks of the masses turning towards Sibylline oracles (pronouncements as gnomic and obscure as Mandleson's Cabinet Office dictats). 'The Johannine tradition,' he writes, 'tells of one warrior-saviour who is to appear in the Last Days, the Sibylline tradition tells of two, but both traditions agree that in those times there will arise an arch-enemy of God, the prodigious figure of Antichrist... His wickedness, though absolute, will be most cunningly masked and this will enable him to establish a tyrannical rule of great strength.'

The Millennium Experience was the first major misjudgement by the New Labour conceptualists. How can Blair, who emerged so powerfully, a sensitive manipulator of national emotion, from the week of public mourning for the Princess of Wales, have been persuaded to give his blessing to the Teflon Hedgehog? Letters and e-mails poured in to the newspapers' correspondence columns before the first conspiracy theory about the crash in the Paris underpass was aired on Channel Necrophile. The two most unpopular concepts in the country were the Royal Family and the Millennium Dome. (They seemed to be twinned in a Daliesque cartoon.) The consensus was: dump the first (tumbrels to Tyburn) and turn the second into a shrine to Diana. Should the secret of the tent be a mummified Snow White cadaver? A demi-waxwork that would be a place of pilgrimage, a Soviet/Byzantine relic in a glass coffin? Take back all the money wasted on this millennial junket, said the tabloids, and initiate a cult of the White Goddess. Build a plague hospital. Do *something*. The disaffection for the Dome was hyped by an unprecedented mourning frenzy. Public grief was contagious, but public anger was contained by paying witness to a real-time funerary procession, from the Abbey to the motorway.

It seems so obvious: a millennium can't be pre-programmed. Whatever happens has to be spontaneous. Time was never going to behave itself as the final privatisation – with Peter Mandelson as (one of his self-awarded titles) 'the single shareholder'. The borough of Greenwich, the old nautical town, is already pimping time in an efficient walkthrough museum and heritage complex. Foreigners can learn how to queue, before being confronted by racks of Dava Sobel's best-selling *Longitude*. They can, if they choose, pay a quid to have a machine tell them what time it is. Thus eroding yet another of the hereditary duties of the British bobby. They can watch the spectral East Greenwich Peninsula glide across a circular table in a darkened camera obscura chamber (the grandfather of virtual reality). They can put an eye to a telescope fixed along the line of zero longitude and check out the great white saucers of the British Telcom reservation on the north shore. They can see how the line fails to pass directly through the Dome.

But in a zone dedicated to the franchising of time, the Teflon Hedgehog is not going to enjoy much of it. Around twenty-five years is a common estimate. What I hadn't grasped, until I was given that figure, was that the Dome would be no more than a mega-budget version of the Rachel Whiteread *House*. 'A mute memorial,' as the artist said, 'to the pathos of remembering.' It's an installation that has been made to disappear. A tolerated obstruction. There's no need to put anything inside it. It's the ultimate art world trophy, a sketch whose existence is confirmed – as a proposal. Building it was the mistake. All that's now required is to enlarge the viewing platform, put the tickets on sale. Let the crowds watch the tent being erected. Let them watch it come down. Then bus them in to see the shadow on the turf where this mysterious object once stood. Sign up the top memory men, fabulists capable of mythologizing an event that never happened.

For most of us, the millennium's future is all used up. It's redundant. Too much emotion had already been invested in a spectacle that hadn't been pre-sold, serialised in advance. It simply occurred one drowsy Sunday morning as the public picked at their bundles of newsprint. There were images that managed to shock, a black metal tangle reduced to vegetable pulp. Flashbulbs in the underpass. After Ballard and Cronenberg, after the hagiographies, the rancid exposures of Jackson Pollock, James Dean, Jayne Mansfield, Princess Grace, here was the symbol that the dying century, with its auto-sex, man/machine hybrids, required. Diana's death was not so much an intimation of mortality for newsbite junkies as a reality fax. Large sections of the population (especially those from Essex and the Estuary) took to the streets, laying siege to swathes of Whitehall, Secret State holdings, privileged real estate. They produced an unprecedented tide of folk art, hand-printed cards, gaudy Xerox tributes, silver balloons, teddy bears, plantations of forced blooms. A glittering cellophane moat around the railings of the royal barracks. The heady perfume of dying wreaths and tissue-wrapped lilies, carnations, roses, chrysanthemums, heaped against the chapel where the body was lying in state.

That's how it happens. Then it's over and we can all get back to the usual small strategies of survival. Trauma is neutralised as product, something you can buy (Elton John saccharine, albums of sentiment), or somewhere you can boast of visiting. Those responsible for promoting the Dome might learn from this episode. They might learn modesty. Tear down the fences, open up the river frontage, let the land run wild. No tent shows, but the sort of tolerated meadows that once existed outside the walls of the city. Somewhere to listen to the riffs of ranters and unsponsored visionaries; soothsayers, however distracted, who understood that this was a place with a long and complicated history, industrial and geological, that would never take its allotted role in the national cartoon without delivering an angry sense of its troubled past and its uncertain future. The Dome was a blind, milk-white eye staring in innocence at a race of storm clouds piling up over Gallions Reach.

Panic on the Peninsula. Outrage in North Greenwich. The gas holder, familiar to motorists skirting the site of what is now 'The Millennium Experience', set ablaze. Flames visible across the river from Beckton Alp to Parliament Hill. 'A man said to have a slight Irish accent said: "This is the IRA. We have planted bombs at the southern entrance to the Blackwall Tunnel. For goodness' sake, do something about it. We want the area cleared."' So Gareth Parry reported in the *Guardian* of 19th January 1979. Bomb carriers, from Conrad's *The Secret Agent* to Paul Theroux's Deptford-based urban terrorists in *The Family Arsenal*, have delighted in targeting Greenwich domes. There is something in the nature of the place, a residue of royalty and privilege and congenital self-satisfaction: the way the old dockside dowager had painted herself up for the punters, while revising her lurid past through shifty tourist brochures. Clap sores revamped as beauty spots. PR operatives delighted in being, at the same time, both economical and spendthrift with the truth. Acceptable glories – the knighting of Sir Francis Drake and Sir Francis Chichester, visits by Samuel Pepys, location work for the latest Jane Austen, or Harrison Ford (more bombs) in *Patriot Games* – are trumpeted, while the dark history of the Greenwich marshes, a decayed industrial wilderness, is brutally elided.

The tongue of poisoned land, a couple of miles to the east of the Royal Naval College (film set, banqueting hall for hire, weddings a speciality), that is being prepared for its tent show apocalypse, has never previously been part of the Greenwich story. The Peninsula, if you check it out on a 19th-century map, is a vestigial tail, a stump known as Bugsby's Marshes. Contemporary hand-colourists, or fakers of the type who now congregate in Greenwich's covered market peddling artfully distressed pages ripped from antiquarian volumes, have tended to leave the Peninsula well alone. Reality, out there, was always in need of a little cosmetic enhancement. Design buffs on the Millennium Experience payroll see the sorry isthmus with its muddy horizons, its earth-movers and excavators, its razor-wire fences and surveillance cameras, as an Arcadian grotto. They have no problem with deferred pleasure. They read the future like a transcendent comic strip. Old Thames is rejuvenated in a Mediterranean blue. There are avenues of potential trees, future forests. Docklands is a garden city, clean, broad-avenued, free of traffic, and peopled entirely by vibrant ink spots. But the 19th-century colourists, busy with miniature orchards on the Isle of Dogs, with windmills, golden sandbanks at the mouth of the River Lea and deepwater docks of a Byzantine blue, baulked at Bugsby's Marshes. The swamp defied their imagination. Its karma was too terrible. They knew the story and knew that any proper human settlement needed its back country, its unmapped deadlands. The Peninsula was where the nightstuff was handled: foul-smelling industries, the manufacture of ordnance, brewing, confectionery, black smoke palls and sickly sweet perfumes. The cloacal mud of low tide mingled deliriously with sulphurous residues trapped in savage greenery; the bindweed, thorns and dark berries on the riverside path.

The Peninsula thrives on secrecy. For as long as anyone can remember much of this land has been hidden behind tall fences. Walkers held their breath and made a wide circuit. Terrible ghosts were trapped in the ground. A site on the west of the Peninsula, now captured by the Teflon-coated fabric of the Dome, had once featured a gibbet where the corpse of some pirate, removed from Execution Dock in Wapping, would be left to decay. Pre-Dome picaresque. A crow-pecked rehearsal for Gerald Scarfe's satiric figurines which will set-dress the great white tent. Executions and bloated bodies washed over by three tides were less a public spectacle (a Mortality Experience) than a ritualised necessity. Distance and difficulty of access blunted the urban mob's appetite for blood. But the inhabitants of the Peninsula were feral inbreeds comfortable with the maggoty underside of history, the prison hulks, the ammunition manufacturers, the skull-hammering intoxification of the South Metropolitan (later East Greenwich) gas works. Much of this land, then as now, was compulsorily purchased to be held in stock for 'future possible expansions'. The Molochs in workers' cottages and burrows, who the rest of Greenwich refused to acknowledge, mutated as they came to terms with the by-products of the gas industry: coal gas, tar, sulphate of ammonia; the trains, the phenol, the never-ending noise (grinding, thumping, whistling, clanging). Here were the ancient fragrances of the soap works; bone crushers, whale-rendering boilers. Manufacturers of artificial manure steamed their cauldrons of salvaged leather, sugar waste and bone-ash. Droplets of sulphuric acid fed the surviving cabbage patches. Even in the 19th century copywriters knew the value of a good tag. The Thames Steam Soap Works traded under this slogan: 'Greenwich the world standard in both soap and time'. Before Amylum UK forced motorists creeping from the Blackwall Tunnel to rapidly wind up their windows, Wilkes and Soames (formerly of Spitalfields) were blanketing the North Kent foothills with the reek of Russian tallow. Prime candles were marketed as 'Greenwich Sperm'. Lamp black from the manure works found its way into locally produced steak puddings. Stinks that have mixed and mingled for generations in increasingly complex chemical combinations now gift unwary tourists with stomach-churning hallucinations, flash-backs to ancient horrors, dizzying premonitions of catastrophe.

In a sense, it was very perceptive of the New Millennium Experience promoters to nominate Bugsby's Marshes as the site for their monumentally expensive folly. Where better to greet the millennium (even if the nominated date is meaningless) than this ravished swamp with its history of plague, pestilence and pillage? The Four Horsemen of the Apocalypse, appearing against the sunset on the rise at Woolwich Road, would look like refugees from a donkey derby on Margate Sands. The millennium is nothing to do with bemused civilians, badgered into celebration and rehearsed spontaneity, being shepherded through zones sponsored by multinational pirates. The millennium is fire and terror, the rising of the dead, judgement before revelation. How tactful of the government planners and their commercial allies to shift the Dome site down-river, away from centres of population, contacts with culture. How cunning to nominate a place that is impossible to reach by any existing means of traffic, other than the crawl through the Blackwall Tunnel (where a single misdirected lorry, trying to pick up time in the fast lane, can get trapped by prophylactic stalactites, and bring London to a standstill).

I was intrigued, when the LRB offered me the chance of another jaunt south of the river, fifteen months on from my original visit to the Millennium Experience building site, to see how work was progressing. I duly reported my shoe size (which hadn't changed much since the previous trip) and the number of my car (nobody penetrates the security barriers on foot), and I looked forward to my Friday afternoon appointment at Gate 1A. It had taken weeks to set this up, but I wasn't surprised when, a couple of hours before I set off for the Blackwall Tunnel, the tour of inspection was cancelled. Deferred satisfaction. Future bliss. That's what this gig was all about. It's a Calvinist package. Suffer now, the worse the better, and paradise will follow. We are being asked to endure the noise, dust, pollution of a 24-hour building site, as vindication for the heavenly pleasure park that is, just, around the corner. It's a long 'just': long enough to give the advertisers and image-enhancers time to whet our appetites, convince us that this Disneyland trade show is something we can't live without. Meanwhile, we must tolerate railways that don't work, public roads with private security barriers, river paths that run up against plywood fences, naked dirt from horizon to horizon, and a quadraphonic Serbian soundtrack.

Denied my excursion, I decided to find out – it was late January, a year before the Dome would open to the multitudes – how the journey across London would feel. This was no epic, a mere five or six miles as the seagull swoops; Hackney to Greenwich, you'd walk it in a couple of brisk hours. (With another hour thrown in to detour recent excavations, schlep the Peninsula path and play chicken on the odd motorway.) How long could it take on public transport? The Millennium Experience copywriters spoke with breathtaking self-confidence of a 'twelve-minute' ride from the centre of town (by helicopter presumably). The Peninsula diggings (a mantle of poisoned soil dumped as landfill in Bedfordshire) promised to act, so the promotional folders told us, as 'the catalyst for massive investment in new transport services'. By which they meant the Jubilee Line, the completion of which was announced for 1996, then 1998, then spring, summer, autumn, and now late December 1999. An interesting white-knuckle ride for the politicians. The line had soaked up, so far, around £3.3 billion, but its apologists (cursing critics as spoilsports) spoke airily of how all major construction projects come in a whisker over budget. Look at the Channel Tunnel, the Limehouse Link. Look at any of the enforced-from-above, late-century civil engineering achievements. Look at anything deriving from the great photo opportunity of the era: Margaret Thatcher, hardhat perched on hard hair, giving her blessing to Paul Reichmann, while they gloat over a scale model of Canary Wharf and the future city of glass.

My spirits were high. The Dome (or 'Doom' as displaced locals spoke of it) was a Bunyanesque target, a revivalist tent show on the far side of a swamp. There was nothing original about this structure, it was a quotation from the Festival of Britain, the 'Dome of Discovery' tricked out with bright ('Van Gogh cornfield') yellow cocktail sticks. Now I appreciated the concept of the Millennium Bug. Here it was, quivering on the foreshore: a white spider-crab. ('It's not a virus, you can't catch it and it certainly doesn't creep around the garden,' according to a breezy government leaflet, *The Millennium Bug: Facts Not Fiction*.) This marine sub-species was a video-grab from Spielberg's *Close Encounters*: an invertebrate alien protected by security fences, strange lights in the night and interplanetary muzak. What the Dome offered was a destination in the deadlands, a magnet for suicide cultists determined to crack the riddle. What exists inside nothingness?

In the mood for a jolly, I risked the Docklands Light Railway. This funfair ride into Canary Wharf and Docklands had been constructed as the cheapest and flashiest of transport options. It was a slightly longer, and much less efficient, version of the ride between the South and North Terminals at Gatwick Airport. As a visionary experience, it had nothing on the long curves, the smooth elevations and courteous, disembodied voices of Chicago Airport's shuttle service. Instead of perpetual motion and a vista of freeways with stretch limos, gargantuan car parks, incoming planes, the DLR offered a stop-start stutter of the unexpected, a preview of bucket-shop time travel.

I walked to Bow Church where I tried to buy a ticket for Island Gardens (so that I could cross under the river through the Greenwich Foot Tunnel). The ticket machines were not working. And Island Gardens was no longer on offer as a destination (deferred satisfaction again). All trains stopped at Crossharbour. Or they would if they could make it that far. The carriages in this unmanned operation (more ghost than bullet train) were occupied, mid-morning, by ticketless school kids who stayed on board for the duration, self-educating through travel. The bonus lay in the aerial views across water to the distant Dome: heavy skies pressing on the spiked Teflon cake. The Dome's achievement, it struck me, was to look definitively unfinished. It would remain a work-in-progress until the day it was dismantled or sold off as an ice rink or storage facility. Seen from Canary Wharf, down the length of a wet grey street (containing nothing but a cab rank and a couple of security men in scrambled-egg vests), the Dome was a spacecraft standing in for all the missing liners and cargo boats from those nostalgic black and white photographs. It was an unoptioned metaphor with its own poet, Simon Armitage, who had been hired to knock up a thousand-line tribute.

Time drifted. The twelve minutes of the virtual reality journey in the brochures was actually the time *between* trains, the time spent enjoying strange termini in which potential travellers are marooned. We were held, without warning, at notable viewing spots (close-ups of the sheds of the transported Billingsgate Fishmarket). And this was fine with me. I was in no hurry. It was pleasant to be able to indulge a good view without the compulsory commentary. Like the school kids, I was reluctant to leave the train when eventually we made Crossharbour. There was no one around to take our non-existent tickets. A bus link carried passengers on to Island Gardens. I didn't have time to wait for the regular service. I walked. A couple of old ladies, huddled against the cruel zephyrs and down-draughts that swept through this *Blade Runner* architecture, remarked, 'You see plenty of those bleeders', as yet another empty link-bus met the train. Meanwhile, they were left waiting, half an hour or more, for the standard Island-inhabitants' cattle-carrier.

I saw, very soon, why the service terminated at Crossharbour. The railway line at Mudchute, looking like the post-detonation bridge on the River Kwai, dropped into an abyss. More pneumatic drills, more compressors, more yellow dust. More present inconvenience to facilitate the great millennial morning. Travel, for the moment, was a brutal obstacle course, which we must endure as our contribution to future bliss. The Island Gardens station, which would in a few months be awash with excited tourists, was now a depressed frontier post with little to offer but badly smudged photos of the dead on commemorative mugs: Freddie Mercury, Laurel and Hardy, Princess Di. 'Small dolls £1.99.' The afterburn of celebrity is a memorial ashtray.

Greenwich is deeply ambivalent about the whole Millennium Experience scam. Most of the place – the area around the Cutty Sark, phase one of the Dreadnought Library of the University of Greenwich – is a building site. And the rest of it is a film set, cranking out heritage for export: crinoline frolics and *The Madness of King George*. I'd barely set foot outside my first second-hand bookshop when I was pounced on by a two-person television crew doing a vox pop on the Dome. There was a man hefting a DVC camera and a woman with a clipboard. After a morning trying to tease a story from inertia and clinical depression – 'What dome?' / 'I'm sorry but we are from the Netherlands' / 'Is that part of Bluewater?' – they were delighted to hit an apocalyptic ranter who didn't actually have foam bubbling from his lips. I let rip in the knowledge that this was a training film for the World Service and would never see the light of day, even if, as seemed unlikely, this pair eventually found their way back to central London.

Greenwich, on the cusp of its new prosperity,

and ready as ever to exploit any opportunity to cram more visitors into a small riverside settlement that was already coming apart at the seams, had tottered towards the kind of New Age, under-the-flyover Portobello-Road gypsy camp that belongs on the South Coast; in Hastings or the warren of junk-peddling back streets around the station in Brighton. The warning signs never change: cards in newsagents' windows advertising Tarot readings and patchouli-oil massage leavened with a rash of charity shops and a plague of cheap books. Here are the dump bins of literacy, 'All for £1' caves where publishers' failed inspirations can crawl to die. Greenwich was bolstered with multiple copies of Anna Pasternak's *Princess in Love*. Dealers in semi-authentic antiquarian bookshops groaned as hustlers with bulging golf carts and child buggies lurched in off the street. 'We've got books. Got 'em all. Cellar's full. Sorry.' Book graveyards are all that remain of Greenwich's punt at civilisation. The theatre, in want of a few hundred thousand pounds of lottery money, has been closed down and repackaged as Landy's Bar.

The river walk, east towards the Dome and the Peninsula, begins at the Trafalgar pub. This was where the famous whitebait feast, enjoyed at the close of parliamentary sessions, took place. They still do a whitebait platter – if you can stare without flinching at those cold grey eyes. I'm not talking about the fish, but the ranks of inscribed black and white photographs that line the walls of the dining room: Harold Wilson, Derek Nimmo, David Steel, Jeremy Irons, Clement Freud, Norman Tebbit, Barbara Castle, Elaine Page, Cecil Parkinson, Nigel Lawson, Robin Day. It's like being compulsorily inducted into a dinner party from hell, a nightmare mix of half-forgotten careerists and political dinosaurs who can't switch off. But there's a great view of the Dome, beyond the bend in the river, a shape that gives purpose to an inadequately defined horizon. On the wall of the pub is a map of the area from the pre-Dome period: 'Guide to the Thames' (by Catamaran Cruises). This improved landscape cuts directly from the Royal Naval College to the Thames Barrier, so that the Peninsula is not merely occulted, it doesn't exist. Geography shifts to suit the strategic needs of the mappers. Territory belongs to those who sponsor the means of transport. If you have to visit the Dome, the local politicians imply, the best way to do it is to stay in Greenwich proper. Enjoy the facilities, the tea rooms, the historical palaces, the locations where notable films were made. Forget the horrors of the journey to the east, the sluggish, overfull buses, the windswept slog through the industrial wastes. 'Discover the Millennium Experience' by dropping in on the Visitor Centre. (The singular tense is accurate. I was on my own in what I took to be the reception area, until I discovered that a desk and a few computers represented the entire pitch.) Play with the virtual reality machines. Purchase the badge or the sweatshirt. Gasp at the scale model. Blush at the hubris of the promotional displays. Giant blow-ups of 'Richard Rogers's original sketch of the Greenwich Dome' are twinned with 'a sketch design for a dome by Sir Christopher Wren'. The puny scale of St Paul's Cathedral is set against the enclosed acres of the tent on Bugsby's Marshes. 'This awesome structure dwarfs the famous domes of history.' But, walking around nautical Greenwich, the first thing the visitor notices is a plethora of domes. Who needs another one, however sonorous with millennial whispers? The pregnant curves of the shadow-catching glass dome at the entrance to the Greenwich Foot Tunnel (a conservatory without ferns and fronds) and the twin domes of the Royal Naval College shame Richard Rogers's shallow dish. It scarcely deserves the title of dome. It is, in fact, a 'cable-net tent', suitable for a trade show or temporary exhibition. Something to throw up fast, without fuss, before getting the caterers in. It's a disposable with ideas beyond its station. So the jobbing artists who have been hired to set-dress the project have found themselves labouring to manufacture a dome that looks like a dome. One of the more sinister tourist knick-knacks on sale in the borough's gift shops is a 'Millennium Countdown Calendar' (published in Tower Hamlets, printed in Hong Kong) with illustrations by Peter Kent. Kent has adapted all the standard tricks – colour enhancement, elimination of the chimney that carries away the exhaust fumes from the

Blackwall Tunnel, weird perspectives puffing the status of the Peninsula - but he can't do much to put a proper curvature into the Dome. It still looks like a junky's time-killing table sculpture from a greasy caff, a heap of icing sugar with twelve match-ends stuck in it. A memento of dead time, a connection who failed to put in an appearance. Kent's sketch for 'The Millennium Dome as viewed from the heart of Maritime Greenwich' cannily plays down the local domes to allow Rogers's distant hiccup its glory as a poached-egg sunset. And all the time – time being the hook – this 'quartz countdown clock mechanism' that has been attached to the calendar ticks away, devouring the remaining days: 286, 285, 284, 283 … A terrible progression for a writer, deadlines vanishing before your fascinated gaze. The mechanism in its complacent little box is as remorseless as Edgar Allan Poe's tell-tale heart and as silent as Conan Doyle's dog that didn't bark. It's the silence that drives you mad.

A second site visit was arranged. A second site visit was cancelled. Indulging my native paranoia, I believed that they must have something to hide. (I'd been told how the LRB's request had slipped through. The Dome office misheard the title of the publication. They thought they would be welcoming a journalist from the London Review of Bricks.) I could fantasise some opinion-forming quango picking my earlier account of a trip to North Greenwich out of the files and reaching for the red stamp: ACCESS DENIED. It was no accident that the Peninsula, with its manned security gates, its boilersuits and hardhats, its earth-moving machinery, its gangs of workers performing a mime of activity, its sirens and flashing lights, behaved like the final, formulaic act of a James Bond movie. Another mad scheme of world domination revealed. Another doomsday weapon defused. Bond movies, up to now, were way beyond North Greenwich's ambitions. The old gasworks had featured in the odd episode of Dr Who and even, curiously, as a set for a British version of Kafka's The Trial. And now, with all this heavyweight sponsorship in the air, the latest Bond epic, The World Is Not Enough, would include a 'high-speed boat chase' along the Thames, from the MI6 fortress at Vauxhall to the Dome. 'Gorgeous Maria Grazia Cucinotta' (aka Cigar Girl) would feature in a product placement orgy, pursued by every means of transport (including the air-balloons that are already drifting across the skyline), to a nail-biting conclusion on the roof of the Dome itself. A brief episode that would budget at around a million pounds.

More mundane methods of transport concerned me. My first excursion concluded with a walk along the river path from Greenwich to the Dome. Maybe that's the Big Idea: persuade enough punters to get their heads down against the cold wind and swallow the rich mix of ammonia and hops and phenol and tar and molasses, the grit from the overhead derricks of conglomerate. A couple of miles of this and they'll be as high as kites, heads ringing from the constant din of drilling, the howling of generators, the fizzing of bright blue Hazchem canisters. Anything, any respite, will be a false paradise. Take in all those rabies notices and the scarlet graffiti left by Russian sailors. Notice the daub that represents Princess Di in tiara outside the alms-houses that shelter in the lee of the Greenwich power station.

Look back at each turn of the river on the charming nautical town, the sun setting across the mud. But forget any notion of keeping to the path. The Dome site finishes all that. A security gate blocks the route towards the Thames Barrier. The West African who guards it can suggest no viable detour. A single pub, The Pilot, stands in the middle of all this dereliction, servicing the work force. (The landlord is sitting on a prime investment opportunity. He's already turned down an offer that would make him a millionaire.) Old maps were useless. I sat with my pint and plotted another attempt on the Dome. I would take a train from Hackney to North Woolwich, cross the river on the free ferry, walk to the Thames Barrier and then join the famous river path that ran, so we were told, all the way to the Cotswolds.

The question becomes: is it possible to reach the Dome by public transport without help from Thomas Cook, a limitless budget and a posse of native guides? At Hackney Central it looked iffy. Hackney, it strikes me, is one of those territories that can't claim a centre. Hackney simply happens. It's caught. Like impetigo. I'm one of the scorned eccentrics who have actually purchased a ticket. The others on the platform live there. A gang of youths, confident in the non-appearance of anything resembling a train, take off down the tracks. And they are right. Masked carriages, stacked with nuclear waste or whatever, rattle through at high speed, but passenger trains are a rumour. There is only speaking-in-tongues feedback from the public address system. The occasional word could be picked out of the acoustic froth: 'apologise ... special bus service ... customers'. That's what we are, ticket-holders or not, customers. But the transport system in Hackney is on a par with the post. You forget about timetables and learn to be grateful if it happens at all. At the end of the last century, it was possible to get into the City in about ten or twelve minutes by train or tram. Now there are only mobs waiting for phantom buses. There's a culture of waiting. Coming down from Lewisham to Greenwich, I discovered people whose lives were based around the time they spent at bus stops. They reminisced, they kvetched. They discussed various ailments and fantasised on their chances of ever reaching a doctor's surgery or out-patients' clinic. And then they went home.

Time passes quite pleasantly in deciphering faded anarchist slogans. The announcer breaks through my reverie to alert us to the fact that there has been 'a sighting in the Dalston area'. Something muddy and wretched, a Balkan troop transporter, or Chernobyl surplus stock, limps in. It will be signed for 'North Woolwich' but it's only going as far as Stratford. Stratford is good. It's one of the grandiose Albert Speer-type wilderness temples of the Jubilee Line. Architect-in-Chief Roland Paoletti has come up with a fabulous glass windbreak, a thing of future walkways and ghostly reflections, that has for the moment been abandoned on a clapped-out railway station, where all the metal benches for the convenience of customers-held-in-transit have been lobbed over the fence onto waste ground.

'All change. This train is cancelled.' By the time a relief train arrived, my journey had taken about half an hour longer than the time required if I'd walked to Greenwich. 'This train terminates at Custom House.' They love that word: terminates. And use it with the relish defence spokespersons give to 'degrade'. 'We intend to degrade their weapons' systems.' Don't think I'm whingeing. It's great. There's been nothing like it since the high days of the Eighties. Total craziness. Lunatic decisions delivered from the top down by a chipmunk with a consensus haircut. Captain Smirk at the controls of the Starship *Enterprise Culture*. 'I am determined to do all I can to ensure that the Dome stands as an enduring legacy for the future,' Chairman Blair announced. A legacy like the South Sea Bubble. The landscape was so strange, so alienated, that you were practically deafened by the noise of conspiracy theorists (Stewart Home and associates) licking their lips. All the old radicals were clawing their way out of the earth to get at it. Fiction was back on the menu. As in a Ballard novel, in something like *The Atrocity Exhibition*, language itself begins to slip. Nouns lose their self-confidence. Proper names dissolve and reform. Dome becomes doom, dune, done. A slow drip of millennial soundbites, repetitions of meaningless statistics. Tyranny by consensus. Send us your ideas and we'll tell you what you want.

The fictive twelve minutes of the brochures should now be read as twelve hours. A family outing to the Dune is a three-day affair. And that's if you live within the sanctuary of the North Circular Road. It's obviously a smart move building a Holiday Inn on the tip of the Peninsula. Nobody will be able to get away. They'll be begging for shelter in riverside dives, pitching their tents in toxic ditches, burrowing into brownfield. Even the free ferry was slow, a single boat operating at weekends instead of the constant shuttle of the working week. But I reached the Barrier without incident. The 'Source of the Thames' was promised as a legitimate destination. 'You are now on the Thames Path National Trail... The Path follows the River Thames for 180 miles from its source in Gloucestershire, through peaceful watermeadows, past historic villages, into the City of London and ending at the Thames Barrier.' Which is a nice promise, but – after a glimpse at the Dome framed between the silver copes of the Barrier, and a half-mile stroll – the connection with the river is broken, and the unwary pedestrian is cut loose on the wild fringes of the Peninsula. Behind the Hope and Anchor pub is a vast storage depot and distribution centre for Sainsbury's. Blue Circle Cement have colonised the stretch that leads to the Dome. Of course, one day, in the dawn of the New Millennium, the Thousand Year Reich of New Labour, the path will be open to all. But for the moment it is fenced off, forcing walkers to detour into the mud and traffic of the building site, where they will be warned off by stern notices – GAS ESCAPE, GAS RELATED EMERGENCY, ELLIS & EVERARD CHEMICALS. There are pictures of ferocious German Shepherd wolf-dogs, red cone roads, and a vista of churned slurry (future parkland). In a few short months, just imagine, all this will be leafy avenues, multi-choice entertainment complexes, and eco-friendly super stores. Sainsbury's are already excavating the base of the Peninsula for a Shopping Experience that will come with its own massive car park, convenient for Dome visitors and motorists on Watling Street, the A20, and all roads from the Garden of England and the Channel ports. The store will open at the same time as the Dome. So, although cars – other than official vehicles, cabs putting down fares, Holiday Inn transients – will be forbidden access to the Dome site, shoppers will be parking in their hundreds to enjoy the benefits of state-of-the-art grocery selection, fruit-picking, aisle-cruising, queuing and credit card bashing.

Will it work? Of course. Will it be ready in time? Certainly. Probably. Maybe. Government is prepared to throw as much money into the hole as it takes (around £758 million and rising). They can't fail. This is their Big Idea. The vision thing made manifest. A celebration of that which is to come (with heavily-edited highlights of whatever has been achieved in the last thousand years of human history that is not offensive to BT, Manpower, Marks & Spencer, Sky, Tesco, McDonalds – and anybody else prepared to chip in the odd 12 million). It's still not too late to buy your own zone. The Mobility Zone will, it appears, be funded by Ford ('product category exclusivity') – whose factory on the other side of the river, in Dagenham, is having to introduce short-time working practices. National Identity (aka Self-

Portrait) has been entrusted to Marks & Spencer, a declining retail outfit struggling (now that there are no longer Eastern block diplomats bulk-buying underwear) to introduce cut-price designer clothes to the high street. The Spirit Zone (aka Faith) has been nothing but trouble, with nobody knowing how to define or exploit it, and a bunch of meddlesome clerics of all persuasions piqued that they haven't acquired the sole franchise. Spirit has been left to the Official Millennium Poet. Simon Armitage, according to Chris Meade, director of the Poetry Society, 'seems just right to us because he has lightness of touch and has written recently about the universe and the stars'. Essentially the Dome is showbiz. Old showbiz, resting showbiz, between projects showbiz: David Puttnam, Michael Grade and sparky Floella Benjamin. Disneyland on-message. The critics have been taken care of with nicely weighted sweetheart deals. The *Mail* along with the London *Evening Standard*, who had combined their anti-Archer campaigns with a series of squibs aimed in the direction of the Dome (Tory revenants both), were offered the contract to market the

Millennium Dome newssheet. Associated News-papers will produce a four-page Dome supple-ment which will be wrapped around its own pub-lications. Opposition from the *Sun* has been mut-ed since its sister company BSkyB chipped in £12 million to sponsor an auditorium, which will be sited next to the Dome.

I couldn't wait to get down there, to see what was happening behind the smokescreen of ru-mour and grey propaganda. Proposals became more fantastic by the day. We were entering the mindscape of Versailles and San Simeon, last-ditch extravaganzas by despots and cortex-collapsing, syphilitic emperors. 'Freeze the Thames.' Call up the barrage, hold back the out-going tide, create an *After London* lake (without acknowledgment to Richard Jefferies). Ice and fireworks. 'As the last spark dies,' one of the visionaries told me, 'the new millennium will break - and, with any luck, lights will go out all over London as the computers crash.' Flood risks and ecological catastrophe have been brushed aside in the thirst for Krug and circuses. I began to feel uneasy about all this. Back in the late

Eighties I'd written a wildly improbable novel, *Downriver*, in which the railways were privatised with unforeseen consequences, in which prison boats were reintroduced; and in which, climactically, the deepwater docks behind City Airport were frozen for an historic pageant, a floodlit storm and blood ceremony. This baroque fiction now read like secondhand journalism. It was spooky to find myself in the same nest of conspiracy theorists as the former DJ and TV chat-show host, Simon Dee. Dee, one of the invisibles whose bulb went out as soon as he was nudged from the magic rectangle, spent years brooding on his fall. Reinvented as an architect, a designer of domes, he settled in Winchester, where he was visited by the journalist Brian Viner. Viner discovered that his luncheon companion was in the grip of 'paranoid delusions'. 'He thinks,' Viner wrote, 'that the British secret service, and possibly the CIA too, tapped his phone, worried by his interest in the assassination of President Kennedy.' After that it got weirder. Dee, it appeared, was commissioned by the Moroccan government to design a dome. The Moroccans spurned Dee's invoice and the contract moved to a cabal of Swiss bankers, who first refused to return his calls and then disappeared. Dee's concept was revealed to the world, years later, as the Millennium Dome. But Simon, like his namesake Dr John, the Elizabethan magus and imperial geographer, was exploited by the Secret State and then abandoned to provincial obscurity. Now it can be told: the Dome represents the consciousness of the lost years of Simon Dee.

Finally, on Friday 12th February, it happened. The photographer Marc Atkins and I were signed in for a site visit. The low-ceilinged reception area was chaos. Dull blow-ups and parched greenery. One girl fielding all the calls, trying to find taxis to get impatient suits out of there, back to the outskirts of civilisation. Flash geezers with metallic briefcases (and matching hair) hung about like arms salesmen in Riyadh. The tour groups were shuffling through like a Comic Relief conga who had misplaced their red noses and sense of humour. They had fancy dress (hardhats in electric blue, gooseberry fool smocks – an infant school painting class) and they talked in hushed voices. They wanted to respond with the proper emotions, with wonder, and pertinent interest in the technological statistics, the canopy of PTFE-coated glass fibre, the seventy-two paired radial cables and the seven circumferential rings, but the noise, the dust, was overwhelming. Our guide was too weary to shout. The keener element in our party clustered around him, notebooks at the ready, shorthanding the boasts ('second biggest, widest, longest... land Concorde on the roof... twelve million visitors') and trying to get their minds around the concept of the Millennial Trinity, how one company could also be three companies (construction, operation, leisure).

We were a low key, second-division straggle of sub-media parasites. The photographers, quickly realising that there was not going to be any defining image, no *Independent* colour spread, took to following each other around. If Atkins dropped back to shoot a sign that announced, NATIONAL IDENTITY, the other lens artist shadowed him. Our guide was impatient with these hireling aesthetes who insisted on going off-piste and hold-

ing up what should be, if he cranked it, a twenty or twenty-five minute gig. I asked the photographer who he worked for and what was his brief. The *Mirror*, he confessed, employed him on the understanding that he stuck to 'people and nothing arty'. If he wanted to be flash, he could do it on his own time and hassle one of the design magazines. Most of the other journos were obviously in rehab or on their way to meet it, trembling burnouts or novices with biro smudges instead of lipstick. One young enthusiast, still notetaking ten minutes in, worked for *The Wharf* (*Canary Wharf's Exclusive Weekly Paper*). Her brief was simple. 'There's a lot of politics involved down here. Don't upset anyone.'

The usual scenario is that critics of the Dome, Dome wets, once they get inside will gasp with admiration. 'I had my doubts, but seeing this, well, I'm gobsmacked. It's awesome. This justifies everything.' (Robert McCrum with his piece, 'Romancing the Dome', written for the *Observer*, delivers the classic revisionist apologia. The Dome was a dollop of tedious, over-expensive crap – 'preposterous behemoth' – stuck in some gulag he'd never dream of visiting, until, flattered by Simon Jenkins, 'the millennial commissar', he agrees to take on the role of cheerleader and literary editor. 'Laurie Lee played the same role on the South Bank in the Festival of Britain, I was hooked.' So, miraculously, the Dome starts to look good. The Dome language, now 'inspired by Samuel Johnson and George Orwell', improves. The fourteen zones are rechristened. Thanks to McCrum, what was once 'Work & Learn' will henceforth – or until the next script-doctor is brought in – be known as 'Work/Learning'. 'The Bodies' has been purged to 'Body'. ('How I stopped worrying and learned to love the Dome' is the unspoken subtitle.) And there'll be more, much more of this slurry as the big day approaches and the pre-millennial parties pick up momentum. Miltonic curmudgeons will be painlessly suborned by superior plonk, freebies and unlimited space in the broadsheets. I was prepared for that, the Dr Who experience, finding the laws of time and space in suspension, beauty locked beneath an unpromising carapace. But, in reality, the building site was everything I anticipated: all the excitement of a slightly dirty circus tent, without the sawdust and the smells. A dull ring set with blockhouses at regular intervals which would eventually contain refreshment areas and toilet facilities. There was also a solitary red double-decker bus. (So that's where they've got to, I thought.) We plodded around the circumference, trying to form a narrative out of a few workmen camping about with bundles of steel rods on their shoulders. The exhaust funnel from the Blackwall Tunnel was masked off, in purdah. Its lip emerging from a hole in the net ceiling. Otherwise there was nothing to focus on, nothing to read beyond a collection of red and white notice boards, hammered in at regular intervals: M,7 WORK / LEARN… M,5 BODY… CONTAMI-NATED AREA. PROTECTIVE CLOTHING MUST BE WORN… YOUR HEALTH, YOUR RESPONSI-BILITY. The big millennial show would take place in the middle of all this: Peter Gabriel and a bunch of trapeze artists. This was what we were paying our lottery taxes for: a bald shell stretched to its limits to accommodate anyone prepared to kick in the necessary millions for a trade stand.

Boots the Chemists would dominate the exhibition space with their inflatable giant (who appeared to have been sculpted from condoms stuffed with glittering sand). A figure that belonged in Las Vegas, soft-selling casino culture.

When it was over, Atkins and I mooched around the river path, walking towards the Thames Barrier to get a few decent photographs. Inside the Dome, the skinhead photographer had lost interest. The light was dead. The visit had climaxed with an ascent onto the roof of one of the blockhouses. A lady journalist, suffering from vertigo, dropped out at this point. The experience had been profoundly depressing. And our attempt at driving back through the Blackwall Tunnel was worse. Even now, in the dog days, the drift of workers leaving the site brought the north-flowing traffic to a standstill. It was backed up from the tunnel entrance as far as we could see; to the heights of the Old Dover Road and beyond. Millennial stasis. The silence after the breaking of the Seventh Seal. Feeder roads across the wasteland were also blocked. A few cowboys lost their nerve and mounted the kerb, skidding off into the muddy paddocks. We followed them, edging and creeping east towards the Woolwich Ferry.

I meditated once again on the bad karma of this site, the sinister back story. Stick a compass in the Dome and make a sweep across the ground, from Deptford to Eltham. It was like a black museum: the death of Christopher Marlowe at the riverside, his bones in St Nicholas's churchyard. Lewisham Station with its straggle of travellers' caravans was offering itself, so I discovered, as one of the gateways to the area. This was where the family of Irish travellers thrown off a flight to the Caribbean, after a riotous mid-air brawl, lived. Seeing the place, you couldn't blame them for spending £15,000 on a winter break. Dogs, men in groups patrolling the yard, occasional enterprises in the black stuff. The single word, RUBY, sprayed on a brick wall. The real Greenwich. Banks of TV monitors on the station platform and a nostalgic red postbox outside with a black and yellow ribbon across its mouth: NOT IN USE. On the scarlet pole of a surveillance camera is another notice: SECURE YOUR VALUABLES NOW! THIEVES OPERATE IN THIS AREA.

As indeed they do. Just down the line in Catford, Mr Smith's Club was the location for the affray that led to the death of Richard 'Dickie' Hart, the arrest of Frankie Fraser and a spiral of revenge beatings and killings that resulted in the eventual break-up of the Kray and the Richardson gangs.

Walking this dark semicircle at the back of the Peninsula, head aching from noise, fumes, overload of facts hoovered up at the local history library in Mycenae Road, it soon became evident that the bus shelter was an outmoded concept. On the long drudge up Shooter's Hill there were no structures offering protection from the weather while you waited for a theoretical bus. The current shelters were austere, minimalist, frames surrounded by shimmering ice-puddles where the glass had been punched out. Citizens were frightened, even on this aspirant-suburban avenue, to wait alone. Windows in the gaunt barracks of Brooke Hospital were boarded over; another 'prime residential site' offered for sale. As I turned down Well Hall Road towards Eltham, the regularly spaced bus stops took on a more threatening aspect. Where else would you find one protected by a yellow-smock policeman? A government employee deputed to patrol a black memorial slab set into the pavement, surrounded by a heap of floral tributes. This tidy dome of cellophane, plain paper and pink paper funnels, marked the spot where Stephen Lawrence was murdered. The protection of a tall pole, topped with a (fake) surveillance camera, had proved inadequate. The memorial slab had been vandalised. Hence, in these sensitive times, the slow-moving copper plodding his tight circuit.

What had happened, I wondered, in the year since my first visit, to the Dome's early champions? The designer Stephen Bayley had resigned, done the interviews and the book, and was now critical of the whole operation. The great New Labour figure most closely associated with the project was the Dome Secretary and so-called 'single shareholder' Peter Mandelson. What was that share worth now? How had the master manipulator allowed himself to be marginalised by something as trivial as a bit of social climbing in Notting Hill, some petty cash borrowed on gentlemanly terms from a wealthier colleague?

Would the Big Idea, the idea which is no idea, a skin with no pudding, deflate without the genius of its most powerful fixer? Stuck in the late afternoon traffic, unmoving in the darkness of Bugsby's Marshes, I began to understand. Mandelson was always months ahead of the game. He could sniff a millennial disaster before the first whiff of the old gas works crept through the foundations of the Holiday Inn. Mr Dome identified himself with the early energy, the reclaiming of dead land, the glorious launch of a fraudulent and boastful folly, but was smart enough to see the extent of the sewage that was about to hit the air-conditioning system. Better to be on sabbatical. Mandelson's break from the stress of government was the equivalent of John Major's convenient toothache at the time of the shafting of Lady Thatcher. A leak here, a hint there, a little gentle self-outing and Mandy was out of the limelight, picking up the sympathy vote, at the very moment when the monster he had unleashed, and gloried in, was about to come spectacularly off the rails. When the dust settled, who would be there to pick up the pieces? Who would oversee the sell-off? No. This must never happen. The Dome must succeed. As soon as I got home, I would put in for a couple of family tickets. I would clear a week or two for the journey, lay in supplies of water, rations of pemmican, and hope for the best.

It was going to be a warm day. The haze was lifting from the river. As I sat on my heels, digging into the damp shingle under Folly Wall, the Dome, reflected across a swift-moving current, began to look better and better. Could this tent really be, as Clive Aslet (author of *The Story of Greenwich*) called it, a 'parasol on the sunny strand of the future'? Should we read some geomantic significance into the claim by project architect Michael Davies (a ginger-bearded cove who dresses from head to toe in red, including a personalised hard-hat and scarlet Soho wellies) that 'the circumference is the exact size of the Avebury Ring'? Exact? Would the Millennium Dome one day be the site of pilgrimage? The epicentre of an astrological cult? Should we start checking out the Erith Marshes for crop circles? I was almost ready to believe it. After all the tortuous journeying, a temper close to affection had developed for this despised and despicable husk. Looking at the Dome, as if for the last time, it began to remind me of something: the shallow curve on the top of a gasometer. The fizzing head on a giant canister of North Sea gas. The upturned canvas saucer, in spite of all my jibes about alien structures, had remained true to the karma of the ground on which it had been erected. The most expensive open-air art work in the western world was a teasing back-reference to the Peninsula's industrial past. Its stretched skin was no more than the bald crown of a clapped-out gas holder, the skeletal armature replaced by a set of natty yellow spikes. References to architectural gems such as the dome of St Paul's cathedral were horribly misplaced. The Dome was entirely self-referential, a metaphor for its own narcissism. Form without function.

I had been lulled, by the lapping water, the dull warmth of a pearly morning, river and sky, into making my treaty with a shape I couldn't bring myself to hate (it was too provoking for that). Now that I would never be required to go there again, I had to admit that – at the right distance –

it had a certain chutzpah. Hadn't it been the perfect target, caught by an amateur video buff, for a bolt of lightning during the recent electrical storm? Wouldn't it be more of a challenge to find something positive to say about a construction that was hated by two-thirds of the population, and a subject of supreme indifference to most of the others? The dandies, the freeloaders, were coming across in droves. If I could conjure up this so-convenient phantom walk across a beach that I hadn't revisited in months, then I could do my best to find virtue in a Millennium Experience that had absorbed the energies of so many of the great and the good. Like everybody else, I could play with virtual reality and settle for what ought to be, rather than what, all too loudly, is.

Select Bibliography

Clive Aslet, *The Story of Greenwich*, 4th Estate, London, 1999.

Norman Cohn, *The Pursuit of the Millennium*, Paladin, London, 1969.

Bill Drummond, 'Breakfast with the Unabomber', from *Annual Report to the Mavericks*, Writers & Film Festival, Penkiln Burn, 1998.

Stewart Home (his clones, avatars & ghosts), *Smash the Occult Establishment*, London Psychogeographical Association Newsletter No. 6, London, Beltaine, 1994.
-- *Isle of Dogs Leyline Bombed*, London Psychogeographical Association Newsletter No. 13, London, Imbole 397.
-- *Run Up to Ritual Murder*, London Psychogeographical Association Newsletter No. 14, London, Beltaine 397.
-- *Nazi Occultists Seize Omphalos*, London Psychogeographical Association Newsletter, Single-sheet flyer, London, n.d.
-- *Say NO to the Millennium*, London Psychogeographical Association Newsletter No. 18, London, Beltaine 398.

Mary Mills, *Greenwich Marsh – The 300 Years Before the Dome*, M. Wright, London, 1999.

Leon Morris, *Apocalyptic*, Inter-Varsity Press, London 1973.

John Pick and Malcolm Anderton, *Building Jerusalem: Art, Industry & the British Millennium*, Harwood, Amsterdam, 1999.

Part of Sorry Meniscus was first published in the London Review of Books on 13 May 1999. The London Review of Books may be ordered through your local newsagent or taken on subscription. For subscriptions please call 020 7209 1141 or fax 020 7209 1151.